WOOD TURNING

BY

E. A. DINMORE

THE LATHE AND ITS ACCESSORIES TOOLS :
TURNING BETWEEN CENTRES FACE-PLATE
WORK : BORING : POLISHING

British Library Cataloguing-in-Publication Data
A catalogue record for this book is available from the
British Library

CONTENTS

Woodworking

Woodworking is the process of making items from wood. Along with stone, mud and animal parts, wood was one of the first materials worked by early humans. There are incredibly early examples of woodwork, evidenced in Mousterian stone tools used by Neanderthal man, which demonstrate our affinity with the wooden medium. In fact, the very development of civilisation is linked to the advancement of increasingly greater degrees of skill in working with these materials.

Examples of Bronze Age wood-carving include tree trunks worked into coffins from northern Germany and Denmark and wooden folding-chairs. The site of Fellbach-Schmieden in Germany has provided fine examples of wooden animal statues from the Iron Age. Woodworking is depicted in many ancient Egyptian drawings, and a considerable amount of ancient Egyptian furniture (such as stools, chairs, tables, beds, chests) has been preserved in tombs. The inner coffins found in the tombs were also made of wood. The metal used by the Egyptians for woodworking tools was originally copper and eventually, after 2000 BC, bronze - as ironworking was unknown until much later. Historically, woodworkers relied upon the woods native to their region, until transportation and trade innovations made more exotic woods available to the craftsman.

Today, often as a contemporary artistic and 'craft' medium, wood is used both in traditional and modern styles; an excellent material for delicate as well as forceful artworks. Wood is used in forms of sculpture, trade, and decoration including chip carving, wood burning, and marquetry, offering a fascination, beauty, and complexity in the grain that often shows even when the medium is painted. It is in some ways easier to shape than harder substances, but an artist or craftsman must develop specific skills to carve it properly. 'Wood carving' is really an entire genre itself, and involves cutting wood generally with a knife in one hand, or a chisel by two hands - or, with one hand on a chisel and one hand on a mallet. The phrase may also refer to the finished product, from individual sculptures to hand-worked mouldings composing part of a tracery.

The making of sculpture in wood has been extremely widely practiced but survives much less well than the other main materials such as stone and bronze, as it is vulnerable to decay, insect damage, and fire. It therefore forms an important hidden element in the arts and crafts history of many cultures. Outdoor wood sculptures do not last long in most parts of the world, so that we have little idea how the totem pole tradition developed. Many of the most important sculptures of China and Japan in particular are in wood, and the great majority of African sculptures and that of Oceania also use this medium. There are various forms of carving which can be utilised; 'chip carving' (a style of carving in which knives or chisels are used to remove small chips of the material), 'relief carving' (where figures are carved in a flat panel of wood), 'Scandinavian flat-plane' (where figures are carved in large flat planes, created primarily using a carving knife - and rarely rounded or sanded afterwards) and 'whittling' (simply carving shapes using just a knife). Each of these techniques will need slightly varying tools, but broadly speaking, a specialised 'carving knife' is essential, alongside a 'gouge' (a tool with a curved cutting edge used in a variety of forms and sizes for carving hollows, rounds and sweeping curves), a 'chisel' and a 'coping saw' (a small saw, used to cut off chunks of wood at once).

Wood turning is another common form of woodworking, used to create wooden objects on a lathe. Woodturning differs from most other forms of woodworking in that the wood is moving while a stationary tool is used to cut and shape it. There are two distinct methods of turning wood: 'spindle turning' and 'bowl' or 'faceplate turning'. Their key difference is in the orientation of the wood grain, relative to the axis of the lathe. This variation in orientation changes the tools and techniques used. In spindle turning, the grain runs lengthways along the lathe bed, as if a log was mounted in the lathe. Grain is thus always perpendicular to the direction of rotation under the tool. In bowl turning, the grain runs at right angles to the axis, as if a plank were mounted across the chuck. When a bowl blank rotates, the angle that the grain makes with the cutting tool continually changes between the easy cuts of lengthways and downwards across the grain to two places per rotation where the tool is cutting across the grain and even upwards across it. This varying grain angle limits some of the tools that may be used and requires additional skill in order to cope with it.

The origin of woodturning dates to around 1300 BC when the Egyptians first developed a two-person lathe. One person would turn the wood with a rope while the other used a sharp tool to cut shapes in the wood. The Romans improved the Egyptian design with the addition of a turning bow. Early bow lathes were also developed and used in Germany, France and Britain. In the Middle Ages a pedal replaced hand-operated turning, freeing both the craftsman's hands to hold the woodturning tools. The pedal was usually connected to a pole, often a straight-grained sapling. The system today is called the 'spring pole' lathe. Alternatively, a two-person lathe, called a 'great lathe', allowed a piece to turn continuously (like today's power lathes). A master would cut the wood while an apprentice turned the crank.

As an interesting aside, the term 'bodger' stems from pole

lathe turners who used to make chair legs and spindles. A bodger would typically purchase all the trees on a plot of land, set up camp on the plot, and then fell the trees and turn the wood. The spindles and legs that were produced were sold in bulk, for pence per dozen. The bodger's job was considered unfinished because he only made component parts. The term now describes a person who leaves a job unfinished, or does it badly. This could not be more different from perceptions of modern carpentry; a highly skilled trade in which work involves the construction of buildings, ships, timber bridges and concrete framework. The word 'carpenter' is the English rendering of the Old French word *carpentier* (later, *charpentier*) which is derived from the Latin *carpentrius;* '(maker) of a carriage.' Carpenters traditionally worked with natural wood and did the rougher work such as framing, but today many other materials are also used and sometimes the finer trades of cabinet-making and furniture building are considered carpentry.

As is evident from this brief historical and practical overview of woodwork, it is an incredibly varied and exciting genre of arts and crafts; an ancient tradition still relevant in the modern day. Woodworkers range from hobbyists, individuals operating from the home environment, to artisan professionals with specialist workshops, and eventually large-scale factory operations. We hope the reader is inspired by this book to create some woodwork of their own.

WHAT THIS BOOK IS ABOUT . .

It has been tritely said that a craft cannot be learnt merely by reading a book, and that the only way to proficiency is the hard one of much practice with failures and fresh endeavours. This is certainly largely true, but there is much also to be said for making use of the experience of others. It can save many hours of wasted labour, and can avoid spoiling a piece of work by pointing out the best method of doing this or that operation. The object of this book is to supply this experience and to show the methods which have proved themselves reliable by the hard test of having been tried out time and again. It is thus primarily a book for the man who is taking up wood turning for the first time, though workers with some experience in the craft should also find in it much that is helpful.

In the work described the reader is taken progressively from simple operations to more difficult turning, and in none of the examples is there a tool operation that has not been previously described in the opening chapters. Generally no dimensions are indicated in these examples because these are details that the reader is better able to decide for himself, partly because of the present-day shortage of timber, and also because it is important that the worker should be encouraged to arrive at pleasing forms by his own volition.

It should be emphasized that, although every effort has been made to describe the various operations as closely as possible, the beginner will almost certainly be dissatisfied with his first efforts. Turning is not a thing that can be learnt in one lesson. But it is also equally true that, as greater control over the tools is acquired, happier results are certain; and with this development will come the creative pleasure known only to the man who, from many failures, has become skilful in using his hands.

THE WOOD-TURNING LATHE

A LATHE for wood turning need not be an elaborate machine. In Buckinghamshire, where much of the turnery for chairs is done, pole lathes were used right up to the outbreak of war. A pole lathe was so-called because a springy pole was used to rotate the work. This was accomplished by attaching a cord to the pole and winding the cord around the work and fixing the other end to a treadle. When the treadle was depressed, the pole was bent down, causing the work to be rotated. The pole, by reason of its resiliency, restored the treadle to its original position, at the same time revolving the work in the opposite direction. The actual cutting was done when the work revolved towards the operator, the tool being withdrawn clear of the work when revolving in the opposite direction. Such a lathe required considerable skill in operation, but much good work was done on these simple machines, and the man who is used to it can work with amazing speed.

Parts of the Lathe. There are few parts in a wood-turning lathe, and their purpose is fairly obvious. They are shown in Fig. 1.

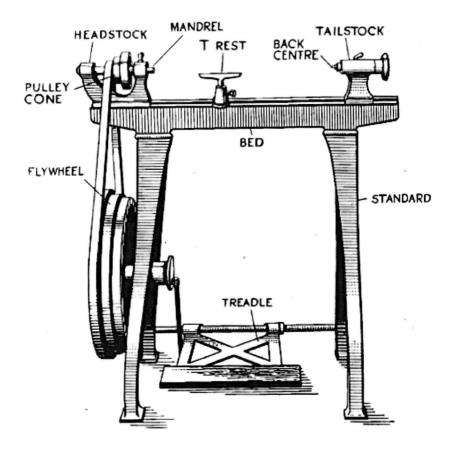

FIG. 1. RELIABLE FORM OF TREADLE LATHE
MOUNTED UPON STAND

This is suitable for both wood turning and light metal turning, boring, etc. An alternative to the treadle type is that fitted with an electric motor. In this the heavy flywheel is omitted, being replaced by a stepped pulley wheel.

Bed. In most manufactured lathes this is of metal and consists of two parallel tracks upon which the tailstock is free to be moved. The latter is thus always in alignment with the headstock. The bed is either mounted upon a standard or, in the case of a power-driven lathe, may be fixed to a bench.

MODERN TYPE OF POWER LATHE MOUNTED ON A STAND

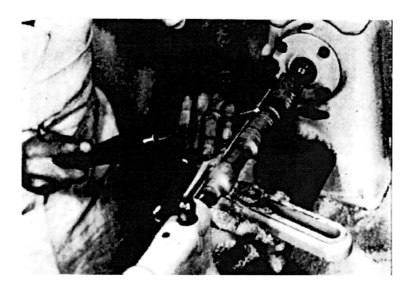

The lathe is the Myford M L 8, with 30 in. between centres and 8 in. swing over bed. Spindle speeds using 1425 r.p.m. motor are 712, 1140, 1780 and 2850.

TURNING WORK BETWEEN CENTRES.

The main roughing is done with the gouge. To finish off flat and rounded surfaces the chisel is used. For softwood both tools should be used at an angle so that they cut the wood rather than merely scrape it. The tool bears on the hand rest, the latter being as close to the work as possible so that it receives direct support. For close-grained hardwoods it is necessary to scrape, and the tool (ground from an old file) is brought up to a horizontal position.

DETAILS OF THE LATHE AND HOW TO CHOOSE ONE

Wood can be used for the bed, providing it is well seasoned.

Flywheel. This is essential in a treadle lathe, and requires to be of fairly heavy construction so that the momentum of the work being turned is maintained during the upstroke of the treadle when no effort is exerted. In a power-driven lathe no flywheel is needed as the drive is continuous.

Headstock. This carries what is termed a "pulley cone," and it will be seen on referring to Fig. 1 that it comprises three steps or pulleys of different diameters. It will also be noted that the flywheel is correspondingly stepped and that the step of greatest diameter aligns with the smallest step of the pulley cone, the arrangement being such that the belt can be slipped from one step to another in order to give different ratios of speed. In turning a softwood, such as deal, a high speed is necessary as otherwise the wood is not cut cleanly.

The necessary high speed can be obtained by driving from the step of greatest diameter to the smallest of the pulley cone. As more power is required when a hardwood is being turned or when the work is of relatively large diameter, a slow speed must be used. In these circumstances the drive is arranged from the smallest step of the flywheel to the largest step of the pulley cone. The speed of a lathe for wood-turning can vary within fairly wide limits. A suitable speed for turning work about 1 in. diameter would be approximately 2,000 r.p.m., while 6-in. diameter work would require about 500 r.p.m. Work which is intermediate of these sizes will, of course, be driven at speeds proportional to those given. It is useful to know these speeds, since if power drive is to be fitted, it is necessary to use a motor which, with a suitable pulley drive, will give these speeds.

The pulley cone is mounted on a mandrel or spindle. In the simplest forms of lathe, the mandrel has a cone bearing at one end, and at the other end a pivot bearing in the end of a threaded stud or bolt which can be easily adjusted to take up any looseness. This arrangement is perfectly satisfactory in practice, but modern lathes have ball bearings with a device for tightening up the cones.

One end of the mandrel projects beyond the headstock and the projecting end or nose is screw-threaded in order that various work-holding devices, or chucks, may be screwed on. The nose in most cases has a threaded or tapered hole, the taper being what is known as a "Morse taper." This threaded or tapered hole is for the attachment of a fork chuck and other fitments, which will be described in a following chapter.

Tailstock. The position of the tailstock can be adjusted according to the length of the work that is to be turned between centres, and the tailstock can be clamped in the required position by a lever or ring nut from beneath the bed.

The back centre is fitted in a tapered hole in a sliding barrel within the tailstock, the hole having a similar Morse taper to that in the headstock mandrel. The barrel, with its centre, can be moved forwards or backwards by suitably rotating the handwheel at the end of the tailstock. In order to prevent any possibility of the back centre moving slightly backwards, owing to vibration, and thus causing the work to become loosely mounted, the barrel can be clamped by the lever the end of which is shown projecting above the tailstock in Fig. 1.

The size of a lathe is designated by the distance of the centres from the bed, the maximum diameter of the work which can be turned by the lathe being slightly less than twice this dimension.

T-rest. As its name implies, it is of T formation, the upper part serving as a support for the tools. This part is adjustable both as regards height and angle with respect to the bed and it can be locked in position by the set screw at the side. The base carrying the T-shaped portion is clamped to the bed by a bolt and nut and it can be adjusted to any angle horizontally with respect to the bed. In order to provide for work differing in diameter, the clamping bolt is fitted in a slot in the base. Thus the T-rest, as a whole, can be fixed in any required position transversely to the bed.

Choice of a Lathe. In view of what has been previously said, the reader may have the impression that a good lathe is a luxury as far as wood-turning is concerned. This is not the case, and if the worker can afford it, he would be well advised to purchase a lathe from a well-known maker. By so doing he will avoid the mechanical troubles that are likely to arise in a second-hand or home-made tool.

In selecting a lathe it would be well worth while considering a type suitable for light engineering. Such a type is illustrated in Fig. 1. Few additional accessories are necessary to enable this lathe to be used for metal turning, boring, etc. The size of the lathe is likely to be determined by the length of the purse, but if the worker can afford a fairly large lathe, so much the better, as it will give greater scope for the turning of such articles as salad bowls, bread boards, etc. Some lathes have provision for such large diameter work, the bed having a gap close to the headstock, but it must be remembered that the power driving the lathe must be increased as the diameter of the work is made larger. For large diameter work a flat belt is less liable to slip than a round one.

As electric power is available to most workers, a motor-driven lathe will avoid much of the laborious work that a treadle lathe involves. If it is intended to instal a power-driven lathe, it is advisable to seek the advice of the makers.

TYPICAL ELEMENTARY OPERATIONS IN
WOOD TURNING

CUTTING A SHOULDER.

The gouge is turned over on to its side so that the lower half of the edge only is used.

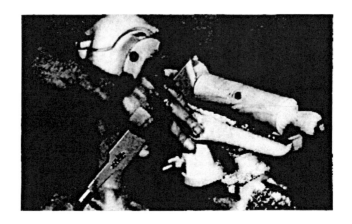

PARTING WITH THE CHISEL.

The tool is held with the narrow edge downwards and a cut made at a slight angle, first in one direction, then the other.

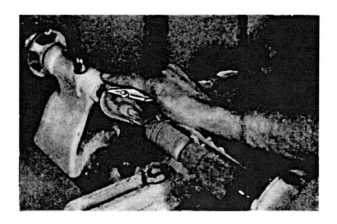

USE OF CHISEL FOR FINISHING.

This tool can be used for finishing all flat and convex surfaces. For concave shapes the gouge is needed.

WORKING OUT SPEED RATIOS FOR POWER LATHES

The second-hand Lathe. If the worker should contemplate purchasing a second-hand lathe, it should be seen that the flywheel does not wobble and that it is in alignment with the pulley cone. Such faults cause endless trouble in keeping the belt on the flywheel, even if this is grooved and a round belt is used. It is also important to look at the pulley cone bearings in order to see that the adjustment is not worn, making the tightening of the cone difficult or impossible. In some of the older types of lathes the treadle bar is mounted between centres formed on threaded bolts. If the threads of these bolts are worn, the bar will work loose and drop down. With the exceptions mentioned, no great accuracy need be looked for in a lathe intended only for wood turning.

Power Drives for Lathes. A power-driven lathe is certainly a great convenience and one of the first questions to be decided is the power of the motor required.

Horsepower of motor. The average worker having a lathe which is capable of turning diameters not exceeding 8 ins. will find that a 1/3-h.p. motor will meet his requirements. It is possible to obtain motors having two windings, one of which gives 1/3 h.p. and the other 1/2 h.p. These windings can be switched in at will, and the arrangement is convenient and economical as it is only on infrequent occasions that the average worker requires to turn large diameters in a hard wood, when the extra power will ensure that the necessary speed is maintained. There is, of course, no objection to having a motor of a higher power than is normally required, as it will be useful to have some power in hand when a heavy load is encountered.

Arranging the drive. If the worker has a treadle lathe and wishes to instal a motor drive without converting to a bench lathe, the drive will have to be arranged so that it is clear of the lathe standards. If space is limited, a countershaft drive could be considered. The most convenient arrangement perhaps is to mount the motor on a bracket bolted to the lathe bed opposite the headstock. Some makers of motors supply special brackets for this purpose.

Control. An A.C. motor of 1/3 h.p. does not require a special starter, and an ordinary 10-amp. switch will suffice. In fact, it is possible to purchase remote control switches for attachment to the lathe. In the case of D.C. motors, however, a special starter is necessary. A motor should not be connected to a lighting circuit, but to a power point.

Drive ratio and speeds. A high speed is required for turning soft woods and in order to obtain greater power when the diameter of the work is almost up to the maximum capacity of the lathe, it is necessary to have different ratios of drive. The average lathe therefore has three speeds. A typical range of speeds for a power-driven lathe is 700, 1,915 and 3,500 r.p.m., but these speeds need not be adhered to closely. A worker wishing to convert his lathe to a power-driven tool will in most cases find that he has to fit a pulley cone to the motor. Fortunately, manufacturers realise this requirement, and it is possible to obtain a pulley for the motor which will match that of the lathe and give the right drive ratios. It is, of course, desirable that the steps of both pulley cones should be such that the belt can be slipped from one speed to the other.

In some cases a worker may desire to make the motor pulley himself, in which case he may be at a loss to know how to arrive at the diameter of the steps. A 1/3-h.p. motor can be obtained which runs at 1,450 r.p.m. and the medium speed of the lathe could equal that of the motor. For example, both steps could equal 4 ins. diameter, in which case the sums of the diameters of the other steps must also equal 8 ins. Suitable sizes could be 5 in. and 3 ins. and 3 ins. and 5 ins.

Given the speed of the motor, the diameter of a lathe pulley step and the speed required, it is possible to arrive at the diameter of the motor pulley step to give the required speed by the following formula:

$$\frac{\text{Speed required}}{\text{Speed of motor}} \times \text{Diameter of lathe step.}$$

To give an example: assuming that the required speed is 700 r.p.m., the speed of the motor 1,450 and the diameter of the lathe pulley step 6 ins. then:

$$\frac{700 \times 6}{1,450}$$
$$= 2.89$$
or say $2\frac{7}{8}$ ins.

If, however, it is the lathe pulley step diameter which is to be known, the formula will be as follows:

$$\frac{\text{Speed of motor}}{\text{Speed required}} \times \text{Diameter of motor pulley step.}$$

ACCESSORIES

IT might be thought that the self-centring and independent four-jaw chucks of the engineer would be as indispensable to the wood-turner as to an engineer, but this is not the case. The chucks mentioned are of course useful to the wood-turner, but the only chucks he must have are the face-plate and the fork chucks illustrated in Fig. 2. As a matter of fact the skilled wood-turner prefers to make his own chucks to suit the work in hand. This will be made clear when specific examples of work are described. As a lathe provides a quick and accurate means for boring holes in metal, it is useful to have a drill chuck and drilling pad, Figs. 2 and 3.

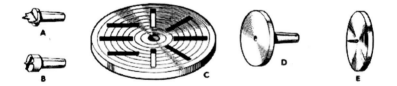

FIG. 2. ACCESSORIES REQUIRED WHEN
TURNING AND DRILLING ON THE LATHE
A. Fork Chuck. B. Cross Chuck. C. Face-
plate. D. Drilling pad. E. Face-plate with
centre woodscrew

FIG. 3. DRILL CHUCK

This fits in the mandrel.

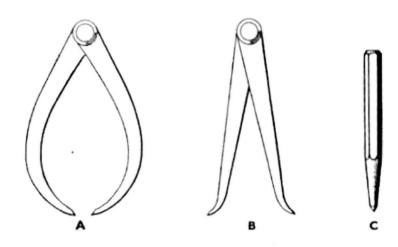

FIG. 4. TOOLS.
A. OUTSIDE CALLIPERS. B. INSIDE
CALLIPERS. C. CENTRE PUNCH

The Fork and Cross Chucks. The fork chuck (A, Fig. 2) has a Morse-tapered shank suitable for fitting in the mandrel of the lathe. There are several sizes of Morse tapers and it is as well to know the size of the taper in the lathe mandrel before obtaining the chuck. This form of chuck is used for gripping work to be turned between centres. Its use is restricted to softwood or work of relatively small diameter since it is inclined to slip and revolve in the end of the work if this is relatively large in diameter. For a hardwood, it is best to use the cross chuck (B, Fig. 2), the cross blades giving a more effective grip.

The Face-plate. For such work as boxes, discs, etc., a face-plate (C, Fig. 2) is necessary. This fitment screws on the nose of the mandrel. The various slots in its surface are for the purpose of receiving screws for the attachment of the work to the plate. As one piece of work may differ from another in diameter, the slots facilitate the positioning of the screws, as will be understood. This type of face-plate can be used in metal turning and the slots are so arranged that special clamps can be fitted for securing the work.

It is useful to have a face-plate fitted with a central woodscrew (as shown at E, Fig. 2) for the easy attachment of the work. It is advisable to make a hole with a bradawl to receive the screw, otherwise there is a danger of the work splitting when being attached to the plate. Obviously, small work or work that is relatively thin cannot be mounted on this chuck.

The Drill Chuck. As a lathe can be used as an effective drilling machine, it is useful to have a drill chuck (Fig. 3) for attachment either to the headstock mandrel or to the tailstock barrel. The drill chuck will be used more often on the headstock mandrel, the work being fed by the tailstock screw. As this exerts considerable pressure it is possible to drill metal without difficulty. It is, of course, important that the work should be held squarely to the drill, therefore it is as well to have a drilling pad (D, Fig. 2) for attachment to the tailstock. This provides a true surface on which the work can be rested while it is being drilled.

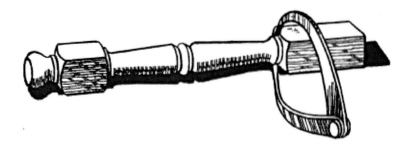

FIG. 5. TESTING DIAMETER WITH OUTSIDE CALLIPERS

FIG. 6. TESTING INTERNAL DIAMETER WITH INSIDE CALLIPERS

Centre Punch. When work is to be turned between centres it is advisable that the centres should be positioned centrally, as far as possible, at either end of the work. If one end is mounted eccentrically it will be clear that unnecessary waste of wood will be caused in turning the stuff truly cylindrical. It is therefore a good plan to employ the method of the engineer and use a centre-punch (C, Fig. 4) for marking the centres. The punch will also be found useful for locating drilling positions in metal.

Measuring Instruments. The only measuring instruments which are essential are the outside and inside callipers (A and B, Fig. 4) and an engineer's 12-in. steel rule. It is also useful to have a 6-in. steel rule for measuring the depth of recesses. The rules will also be required for testing the flatness of surfaces. The method of using the two forms of callipers is shown in Figs. 5 and 6. Fig. 7 shows how the outside callipers are set to a measurement. If it is required slightly to reduce a setting of the callipers, one of the legs can be tapped lightly on the lathe. By holding the callipers upright and tapping the hinge, the setting can be increased.

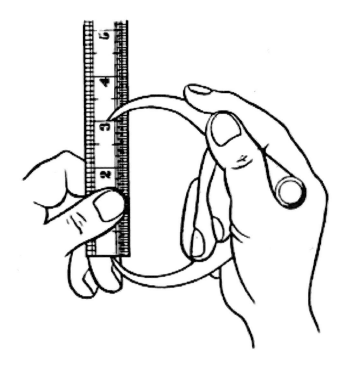

FIG. 7. SETTING OUTSIDE CALLIPERS TO SIZE

WOOD-TURNING TOOLS AND THEIR USE

AS far as the turning of softwoods is concerned, few tools are necessary; in fact, they may be limited to a 3/4-in. gouge and a chisel of similar size. With these tools a skilled turner is able to do a variety of work, including hollow ware. It is helpful, however, to have a 3/8-in. gouge and a 1 1/2-in. chisel in addition to the tools mentioned.

Gouge and Chisel. These tools are shown in Fig. 8. Although the names of these tools will be familiar, they differ considerably from the corresponding tools used by other woodworkers. It will be noted that the edge of the gouge is rounded and bevelled as shown in Fig. 9. The chisel is bevelled on both faces as illustrated in Fig. 10 and its edge is splayed.

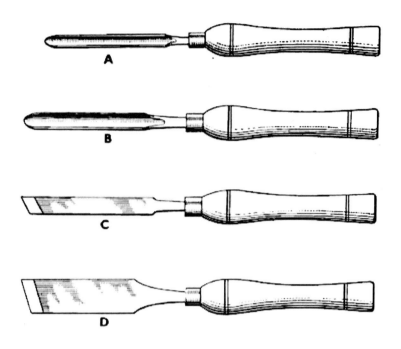

FIG. 8. TURNING TOOLS

A and B show gouges, whilst C and D are chisels.

SHARPENING AND CHOICE OF TURNING TOOLS

Owing to the open grain of a softwood, these tools are used primarily as cutting tools. The gouge is employed for roughing down and working hollow curves, and the chisel for levelling ridges and producing a finish to a surface. If the edge of the chisel is applied to the work so that it is parallel to the fibres in more or less a scraping action, a rough surface will result. In some instances, however, a scraping action is necessary, and in these circumstances an ordinary chisel can be used. For separating or "parting-off" work, a 1/4-in. or 1/8-in. joiner's chisel will answer satisfactorily.

FIG. 9. HOW GOUGE IS SHARPENED

FIG. 10. SHARPENING OF CHISEL

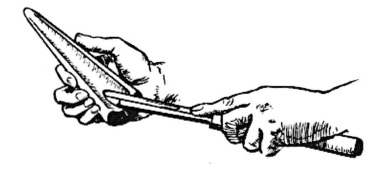

FIG. 11. SHARPENING GOUGE WITH TAPERED OILSLIP

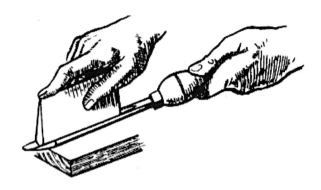

FIG. 12. REMOVING THE ROAFE OR FEATHER
EDGE WITH OILSLIP

FIG. 13. SHRINKAGE TENDENCY OF TIMBER

The heart wood should be avoided for
turning.

FIG. 14. MARKING CENTRES AT THE ENDS

FIG. 15. CORNERS TAKEN OFF BEFORE
MOUNTING BETWEEN CENTRES

Sharpening. No good work can be done unless the tools are sharp, and further, less effort is required when using tools that are really keen. The gouge, by reason of the shape of its cutting edge, is a little difficult to sharpen at the first attempt, as care must be taken to see that the edge is sharp not only at the end but also at the sides. In fact, the whole of the edge must be sharp. The sharpening of this tool is best done on an ordinary oilstone placed at right angles to the position usually assumed when sharpening an ordinary chisel. The gouge is traversed backwards and forwards from one end of the stone to the other, and at the same time given a semi-rolling motion.

Some wood-turners prefer to use a tapered India oilslip for sharpening the gouge, the method of its use being shown in Fig. 11. The roafe or feather edge produced in sharpening is removed with an oilslip in the manner shown in Fig. 12. In order to get a really keen edge to the tools, a strop should be used. This comprises a short strip of buff leather which has been treated with a mixture of emery powder and russian tallow. The strop is similar to that used by wood carvers. The chisel is sharpened in a similar manner to that employed in sharpening an ordinary chisel.

First Use of the Gouge and Chisel. Workers living in the country are fortunate in that they can frequently obtain short lengths or billets of wood. They should, of course, be allowed to dry before being used. It might be thought that a piece of timber cut from a tree would be ideal for turning since it is already roughly circular and but little turning would be required to make it truly cylindrical. But, unfortunately, a piece of branch or stem contains the pith or heart which is often soft wood in which it is difficult to get the fork chuck to grip properly. Further, timber shrinks in the direction of the annual rings, which often results in radial spilts as shown in Fig. 13. It is therefore advisable, when choosing wood for turning, to avoid the pith or heart.

Turning between Centres. In order to gain practice in the use of the tools, a beginner cannot do better than to attempt the turning of a cylinder. A softwood such as deal should be used, although it is more difficult to turn than a hardwood, since if the work is spoilt the waste will be less serious than if a hardwood were used. Further, if a softwood is mastered, no difficulty will be experienced with a hardwood.

Assuming that the lathe will take 12 ins. between centres, cut a 12-in. length of 2-in. by 2-in. straight-grained stuff and plane each face. There is no need to get it precisely square. At each end draw the diagonals and describe a circle equal to the required finished diameter as shown in Fig. 14. Next, reduce the stuff to roughly octagonal form as in Fig. 15. The circle at each end will give the beginner a guide as to the amount which can be removed from the corners, thus avoiding reduction beyond the required finished diameter. This done, make a small depression at each end with the centre punch at the intersection of the diagonals.

Chucking the Work. In order to mount the work, the fork chuck is fitted in the headstock mandrel and the work is pressed on to the point of the chuck, the indentation made by the punch serving to centralise the fork. The back centre is fitted in the punch mark in the other end. This done, lock the tailstock to the bed and turn the mandrel handwheel so that it forces the work further on to the chuck. It will now probably be found that the work will not easily revolve, in which case loosen the back centre slightly, but not sufficiently to cause end play. If the adjustment is satisfactory, the tailstock mandrel should be locked against further movement. If a hardwood is being mounted, it is advisable to make saw-cuts to receive the blades to the cross chuck.

Before proceeding to revolve the work, a drop of oil should be placed on the back centre. Next place the T-rest as close to the work as possible, as shown in Fig. 16. As the T-rest will probably be less in width than the length of the work, it should be positioned towards one end of the work and moved along, as the work progresses. The height of the rest should be such that the cutting edge of the tool is slightly above the centre of the work as indicated in Fig. 17.

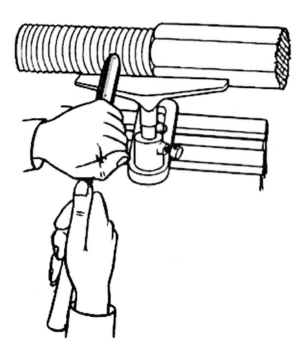

FIG. 16. HOW GOUGE IS GRIPPED FOR
ROUGHING DOWN

Hold the tool firmly as it may otherwise be wrenched from your grasp. Move it steadily along at an even speed and try to keep the diameter constant throughout.

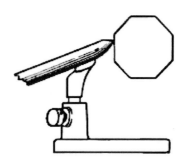

FIG. 17. RELATIVE POSITIONS OF TOOL, T-REST,
AND WOOD BEING TURNED

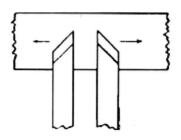

FIG. 18. LEFT- AND RIGHT-HAND FINISHING
CUTS WITH THE CHISEL

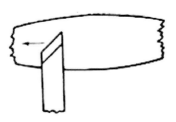

FIG. 19. CUTTING DOWN-HILL WITH THE
CHISEL

FIG. 20. FORMING A SHOULDER WITH THE GOUGE

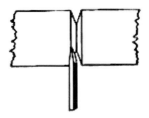

FIG. 21. PARTING WITH THE CHISEL

Using the Gouge. The gouge, which is used for removing the greater part of the waste wood, or roughing down, is gripped as shown in Fig. 16. The tool should be firmly held, otherwise there is a danger of its digging in and being wrenched out of the hands. It is to enable this firm grip to be obtained that the tool is given a long handle. Before attempting to make a cut, try treadling the lathe, which should be run at its highest speed for soft wood. Whilst the work is revolving (which should be towards the worker) endeavour to traverse the tool from one end of the rest to the other at a slow, even speed. To one who has not used a lathe before, this will not be easy, but with a little practice it will be accomplished automatically. At first, take a very light cut moving the tool steadily across the work. Even though the work is being roughly shaped at this stage, effort should be made to keep the diameter fairly even throughout. Having reached this stage, try turning the gouge first on one side and then the other, according to the direction of traverse. It will now be found possible to produce a surface that is almost smooth.

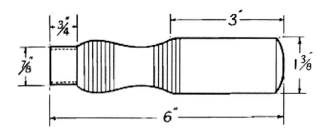

FIG. 22. HANDLE FOR 1 1/2-in. FIRMER CHISEL

The Chisel. When the work is within about 1/8 in. of its finished diameter, the chisel should be used. This is hot an easy tool to handle, but if it can be remembered always to use the centre part of the edge, and never to allow the point to touch the work, its use should not prove too difficult. It will be obvious that if the diameter of the work is relatively large, difficulty will be experienced in preventing the corners of a 3/4-in. chisel digging in. This difficulty can be overcome by using the larger chisel. The position of the edge, according to the direction of traverse, is indicated in Fig. 18. If used correctly, it will be found that a continuous shaving will be removed and that a smooth surface will result. In fact, the finish should be so good that the application of glasspaper is unnecessary.

At this stage, the outside callipers should be used to test the diameter. These are set to the required dimension and lightly applied to the work at several points. A simple expedient for assuring that a cylinder is of equal diameter throughout, is first to turn a small portion of each end down to the required diameter making sure that both diameters are similar. Then remove the work from the lathe and plane one corner down to the turned portions. The work is finally re-chucked and turned down until the planed surface just disappears.

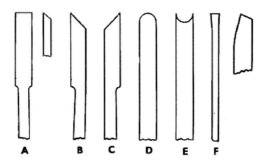

FIG. 23. TOOLS USED IN TURNING HARDWOOD
A. Chisel. B, C. Bevelled chisels. D. Round-nose tool. E. Hollow-nose tool. F. Parting tool.

If a measure of success has been achieved in turning a cylinder, the worker should try curving or tapering the ends as shown in Fig. 19. This will be found no more difficult than turning the cylinder providing the point of the tool is kept clear of the work.

A Shoulder. The next step is to try working a shoulder, Fig. 20. To do this, the gouge is turned on its side, as previously described, so that the lower half only of the edge is used. The tool should be traversed to the left and the work completed as in the case of the cylinder. At this stage "parting-off" should be tried. This is done by turning the chisel on its narrow side and producing a "V" shaped groove by cutting first on one side and then the other, using the lower corner of the tool (Fig. 21).

A Chisel Handle. After a little experience with a softwood, the worker should try turning a chisel handle in a hardwood, such as beech, birch, or ash. This will involve no tool operations other than those previously described. Fig. 22 gives the dimensions for a handle for a 1 1/2-in. chisel. An excess of 3/4 in. at each end should be allowed for parting-off. After punching the centres, the depression at the ferrule end should be drilled deep enough so that when the finished handle is parted off, a central hole will be available. Before mounting or chucking the work, it is a good plan to slip the ferrule over the back centre and to chuck the work so that the ferrule end is towards the back centre. This will enable frequent tests to be made with the ferrule as the pin for the ferrule is turned, and enable a good fit without the necessity of removing the work from the lathe or using the callipers. As before, the stuff is made truly cylindrical throughout its length. One end is then stepped down for the ferrule. This reduced end can be very slightly tapered so that the ferrule can be wedged on.

The curved part can be shaped with the gouge. The beginner will probably have difficulty in getting a smooth finish at the bottom of the curve and in this first effort may have to resort to glasspaper, but if possible its use should be avoided. The rounded end is formed during the parting-off operation. It is inadvisable completely to part-off the work in the lathe; the final removal of the waste should be effected by a tenon saw. Any roughness left by the saw can be removed with glasspaper.

The hole for the tang should be drilled on the lathe. The drill is fitted in the chuck, and the wood held against the back centre. In this way the drill virtually becomes one of the centres. The work is gradually fed forwards until the required depth is reached.

In order to ensure the firm attachment of the ferrule, an indentation can be made on its side with the centre punch. If it is desired to make the slight circumferential grooves or scratches, this can be done by pressing the lower corner of the chisel lightly into the work.

Tools for Hardwood Turning. When proficiency has been obtained in the use of the gouge and chisel, there will be most likely a desire to turn useful and pleasing articles in hardwood. The worker will then find a few essential tools for hardwood turning helpful. Those that will be found most useful are shown in Fig. 23. The bevels of the chisel and parting tool are shown in the fragmentary views. The other tools are bevelled similarly to the chisel. All of these tools are held level on the T-rest in line with the centre of the work. For roughing out hardwood, the round-nose tool is used; so also is the gouge, but it will be found best to use the special hardwood chisel for finishing a cylindrical surface. The edge should not be traversed squarely to the work but slightly inclined so that the leading corner is just clear of the work. This will result in a smooth surface free from ridges. When taking a finishing cut with the round-nose tool on a hollow surface, the tool should be traversed slowly and lightly without pause, otherwise it will leave tool marks.

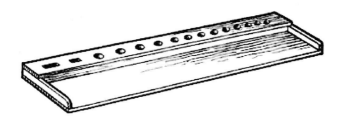

FIG 24. HANDY TOOL RACK AND TRAY

Although the hollow-nose tool is intended for cutting beads, its use includes any convex surfaces of similar curvature to that of the tool, or slightly smaller. With a little practice, however, beads or convex curves of varying size can be worked with the chisel. A square projection is worked first of all, then the corners are chamfered, and finally the chisel is steadily swept round to form the required curvature. Every care should be taken to get the angles at the base of the curve sharp and clean. The finish will be given by the careful use of glasspaper.

A Tray and Tool Rack. It is useful to have a tray at the back of the lathe on which tools, measuring instruments etc. can be placed when required for immediate use. A suitable tray combined with a tool rack is shown in Fig. 24. A good position for a lathe is opposite a window having a north light, and the tray can be supported by brackets fixed to the wall.

TURNING MORE DIFFICULT WORK
BETWEEN CENTRES

IN turning a single article such as a tool handle, it is of no great consequence if the resulting shape is not exactly as intended. In the process of the work, the tool may have dug in or too much material been removed, and to eradicate the defect the shape has had to be altered slightly.

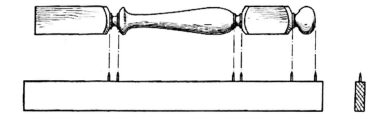

FIG. 25. TEMPLATE FOR MARKING OUT
REPETITION TURNED WORK
Panel pins are driven into the edge of a lath
at the more important members.

Repetition Work. In turning a set of legs for a small side table, for example (Fig. 25), it is advisable to make a full-size drawing of the profile of the turning and from this prepare a template (Fig. 26). In order that the legs should be identical, as far as possible, it will be found useful to make up a marking-out template as shown in Fig. 25. This comprises a strip of wood on which the position of the various members of each turning is marked by panel pins driven into the edge of the strip, the heads being filed off and the ends sharpened.

As in the example of the chisel handle, the work is first turned cylindrical, removing as little wood as possible. The marking-out template is then applied as the work is revolved, thus scratching on the circumference the position of the members. The next step is to rough shape the leg as shown in Fig. 27 by using the parting tool, leaving the diameters a little full for finishing. It is, of course, necessary to make frequent tests with the outside callipers and to make light cuts as the work nears the required diameter. The leg is then further rough shaped with the gouge (Fig 28), taking care not to cut beyond the required size at any point. As before, sufficient material should be left for finishing.

The corners *a* are removed by using the gouge on its side. Care should be exercised in this operation, otherwise the fibres will split out and the only remedy will be to resort to the glue pot. On completing the roughing down, the finishing is effected as shown in Fig. 29, using the two sizes of gouges and chisel as shown. In shaping the quick convex curves, care must be entirely parted off in the lathe, the separation being done with a tenon saw when the work is removed from the lathe.

Chuck for Repetition Work. If four legs only have to be turned, it is not much trouble centring each for chucking in the lathe, but if a number of legs or other turnings are required, all of which are to be turned from square stuff of one size, it is handy to have a chuck as shown in Fig 30. This consists of a piece of wood screwed to the face-plate taken to use only the lower corner of the chisel. On completing the turning, the waste at the back centre should not be and having a central square hole into which one end of the stuff to be turned is fitted.

FIG. 26. TEMPLATE OF PROFILE FOR OFFERING UP TO TURNING

FIG. 27. FIRST STAGE IN ROUGHING OUT THE LEG SHOWN IN FIG. 25

FIG. 28. FURTHER STAGE IN ROUGHING OUT THE LEG

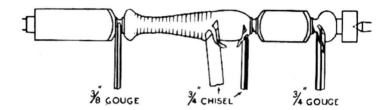

FIG. 29. HOW GOUGES AND CHISELS ARE USED
FOR FINISHING OFF THE LEG

FIG. 30. WOOD CHUCK MADE FOR REPETITION
WORK

FIG. 31. BACK STAY

The Back Stay and its use. In turning work which is long and slender, such as a baton for a music conductor, it will be found that the work will tend to bend under the action of the cutting tools, making the turning of the mid portion of the work most difficult if not impossible. The trouble can be overcome by the use of an additional support for the work, termed a "back stay." It is shown on Fig. 31, the manner of its use being illustrated in Fig. 32. A back stay should be cut from a piece of hardwood, such as beech, the thickness being about 7/8 in. Instead of a V notch, a semi-circular recess can be used, and the notch or recess is cut to suit the work in hand. In order to position the back stay accurately with regard to the lathe centres, it is secured in the gap in the lathe bed by a wedge.

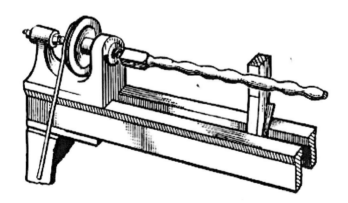

FIG. 32. HOW BACK STAY SUPPORTS THE WORK
The wedge holds the back stay in the lathe
bed.

FIG. 33. TURNED CHAIR LEG WITH CLUB FOOT

In turning long and slender work, it is best to have the stuff well in excess of the finished diameter. By so doing, a central portion can be turned truly cylindrical without difficulty. The back stay is then adjusted and fixed so that the cylindrical mid portion runs in the notch or semicircular recess. In order to avoid undue friction, tallow should be applied to the cylindrical portion. Turning can now proceed on either side of the back stay and, when completed, the back stay can be shifted to a new position, thus enabling the original cylindrical portion to be finished.

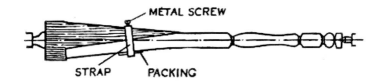

FIG. 34. HOW SPLAYED LEG IS HELD IN LATHE
BY MEANS OF JIG (FIG. 35)

Turning Club-foot Legs. It is a comparatively simple task to turn a chair leg having a club foot (Fig. 33). The stuff is squared up in the usual way and the centres marked. In this case, however, a line is squared across the end where the club foot is to be turned. The work is then mounted between centres with the end which is to have the foot towards the tailstock. The work is then turned cylindrical and the club foot shaped, leaving a slight hollow on the shank side of the foot. The work is then removed from the lathe and re-chucked with the back centre in a new position on the squared line about 1/4 in. or 3/8 in. from the original centre, the centre at the headstock end being as before. The shank of the leg is then turned, with the result that the shank portion towards the foot is eccentric to the latter. It may be a little difficult to turn the curves at the foot so that they flow nicely into one another and it is probable that a little finishing will have to be done by hand with a rasp and glasspaper.

FIG. 35. JIG USED FOR TURNING SPLAYED LEG

Turning a Shaped Chair Leg. In some cases the shape of the work does not permit of one end being centred in the usual way, an example being a shaped chair leg. The method of working in such cases is to mount the splayed portion in a jig as shown in Fig. 34, the jig being illustrated in Fig. 35. The attachment of the jig is effected by a metal strap, formed from strip iron of sufficient thickness to allow of its being drilled and tapped to take a metal screw when the ends of the strap are bent upon themselves. The screw enables the strap to be tightened on the work. It is as well to insert a strip of wood between the strap and the work in order to prevent the latter being bruised. Where the end of the work butts against the jig, a wood screw is fixed into the jig with its head projecting. This is filed to a point, which is driven into the work, thus holding the jig in alignment with the work.

FACE-PLATE WORK

THE turning of hollow ware and wheels is done on a face-plate or chuck, the tailstock being moved back as far as possible. A chuck commonly used for this kind of work is the form having a central wood screw.

Mounting the Work. The face-plate, however, can be used for all kinds of hollow ware by screwing to it a piece of wood (*a*) Fig. 36, made roughly round or octagonal. Care should be taken to see that the screws do not project from the surface. On this piece of wood is glued paper to which the work (*b*) is also glued. When the turning is completed, the finished article can be easily removed by inserting the edge of a chisel in the glued joint and gently levering. If the work is thin, it is advisable to insert the chisel edge on the end grain side of the work, otherwise there is a danger of its splitting. A little paper will be found adhering to the work, but this can be removed by glasspapering.

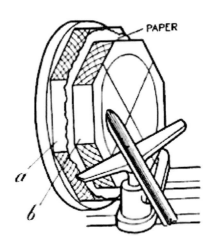

FIG. 36. FACING A SURFACE, THE WORK
MOUNTED ON THE FACE-PLATE

Note that the work is glued to block fixed to the face-plate
with screws. The paper between enables it to be removed
easily.

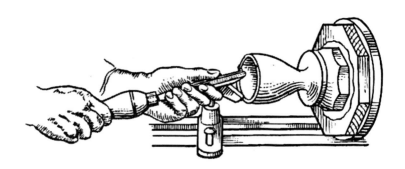

FIG. 37. HOW WOOD IS MOUNTED IN THE
LATHE WHEN TURNING AN EGG CUP

When turning hollow ware, it is best to arrange the grain so that it is parallel with the axis of the article being turned, that is to say, the hollowing-out is done in the end grain. If the grain is arranged the other way, there will be two diametrically opposite points on the external and internal diameters where the tool will be cutting down hill, so to speak, against the fibres, and it will be found difficult to obtain a smooth surface at these points. This trouble will not arise if the turning is done across the fibres.

Prior to mounting the work, the diagonals are drawn to mark the centre and the material is made roughly octagonal. In order to centre the work, the tailstock is moved up and the wood is positioned so that the back centre aligns with the centre of the work. The centre is now advanced by turning the tailstock handwheel which will result in the work being centred and at the same time clamped whilst the glue is setting.

Facing a Surface. Before attempting hollow work, the worker should try facing a surface. It is a good plan to start practising on the wood facing of the face-plate, as its surface should be true before the work is mounted. If, however, the wood facing has been cut from a piece of flooring, it will be found to be fairly true and the need for truing will not arise. If any work has to be done on the wood facing, it is as well to see that there is no possibility of the tool running into the points of the fixing screws. For facing, the T-rest is positioned as shown in Fig. 36, and the gouge is presented to the work so that it is turned slightly on its side, thus using the cutting edge nearest the worker. The tool is traversed from the centre outwardly. If this is done carefully, an almost level and smooth surface can be obtained. To finish the surface, the chisel can be used by traversing the edge across the work, the tool being slightly inclined upwardly. The surface should be tested from time to time with a straight-edge. If glasspaper is used, it should be wrapped round a rubber.

Turning an Egg Cup. This affords excellent practice before attempting something more ambitious. A softwood, such as American white-wood, should be used for the same reasons as were given when the turning of a cylinder was described.

HOW WORK IS TURNED WHEN HELD ON FACE PLATE

SHALLOW BOWL TURNING.

The tool is held on its side as it enters the wood and is given a sort of rocking movement as it passes along to the wood. *The lathe is the Myford M L 8.*

The wood is prepared and mounted as previously described, but if the worker has a screw chuck, this can be used. The work should be mounted so that the grain runs parallel With the axis, as indicated in Fig. 37, and it is important to see that the end to be secured to the chuck is as square as possible.

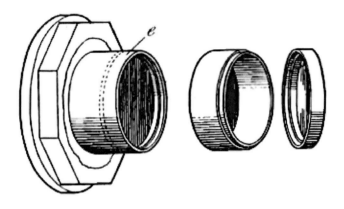

FIG. 38. SMALL TURNED BOX AND HOW IT IS
MOUNTED

The outside shape is turned first using the gouge and chisel, the latter tool being used on the gentle curve. As the work projects considerably from the face-plate without support at its distant end, it is as well to bring up the back centre to support the end whilst the outside shape is being turned. If a single article is being made, the worker should depend on the eye to obtain a pleasing shape, but if a number of similar articles are to be produced, it is helpful to have a template in order to secure uniformity. In the case of an egg cup, the beginner is advised to make a template from card-board, for getting the correct inside shape.

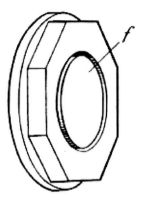

FIG. 39. RECESS IN BLOCK FOR FACING LID

On completing the outside shape, the tailstock should be moved out of the way and the T-rest positioned across the bed of the lathe, as shown in Fig. 37. The first step is to face the end, but there is no need to obtain a level surface. The gouge is then turned on its side and held squarely to the work, the back of the tool being towards the worker. The point or middle of the edge is then brought to the centre of the work and gently pressed in. This will produce a conical recess. The recess is enlarged by using the gouge with its hollow side upwards, as shown on Fig. 37, the edge being slightly above the centre of the work. Only a very light cut is taken and, as the tool advances into the work, the hand holding the handle of the tool is lowered; at the same time, the tool is turned so that the hollow side moves clockwise. At the top of the cut, so to speak, the tool will be almost inverted. The tool, in fact, is given a rolling motion, and if this is done properly, little shavings will curl from its edge and no trouble will be experienced from the tool digging in.

As the hollowing-out reaches completion, the T-rest should be moved to one side and the template inserted. This will indicate where further wood has to be removed. Success will probably not be attained in the first attempt to turn the inside of an egg cup, but the knack in using the gouge will come with practice.

In parting off, it is important to see that the bottom of the egg cup is level. In fact, it is better to make it slightly hollow. The worker may find it easier to use an ordinary 1/4-in. chisel held level with the centre for parting off. In order to prevent the sides of the tool binding, the groove should be slightly widened as the cut deepens.

From time to time the problem will arise as to how a piece of work should be mounted for a particular operation.

Turning a Box. For example, in turning a box as shown in Fig. 38, the work is mounted as in the turning of an egg cup, sufficient material being allowed for the box and its lid, which is turned with the box and afterwards parted off. In this case, it is desirable that the bottom of the box and also the top of the lid should be faced. This may be done by removing the work from the block of wood on which it is mounted and forming a recess in the block, Fig. 39. This should be carefully done so that a cylindrical projection *f* is made on which the box and also the lid will tightly fit. If the fit is too tight, there is a danger of the work splitting.

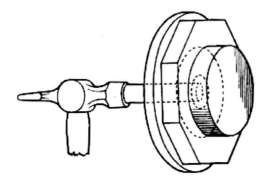

FIG. 40. REMOVING THE WORK FROM THE CHUCK

The frictional grip should enable the surface to be finished with glasspaper wrapped around a rubber or piece of wood. Before mounting the work, a central hole should be made in the block to simplify the removal of the work by lightly tapping a peg of wood inserted in the hole as shown in Fig. 40. The face-plate, of course, is removed from the mandrel for this operation. If the surfaces are to be faced with a tool, the groove in the block should be made deeper. This applies more especially to the box. Obviously only a light finishing cut should be made.

FIG. 41. LONG TURNED BOX

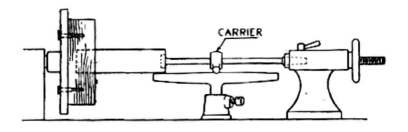

FIG. 42. BIT HELD IN TAILSTOCK MANDREL
WHEN BORING

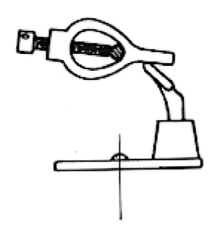

FIG. 43. CARRIER PREVENTS BIT FROM
REVOLVING

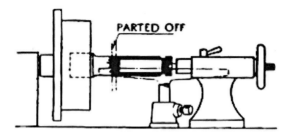

FIG. 44. CAP TO SUPPORT OVERHANGING END
WHEN TURNING OUTSIDE OF BOX

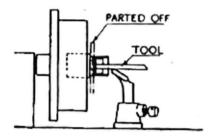

FIG. 45. TURNING LID AFTER MAIN PART OF
BOX HAS BEEN PARTED OFF

Deep Box. The turning of a box where the length is perhaps three times its diameter (Fig. 41), requires a different method of chucking to that used for the shallow box. Unless the work is very rigidly held in the chuck it will be found difficult to hollow out and to secure a uniform diameter. In such circumstances it is best to bore out the interior with a drill or bit, preferably a Forstner bit as this has no gimlet point, and consequently no central hole will be formed at the bottom of the bore. The material for the box should be long enough to permit both the box and its lid being turned from the portion projecting from the chuck, allowing about 1/2 in. for parting-off the box, and a further 1/2 in. for separating the lid.

The material is first turned cylindrically between centres, the diameter being a little full. In this case, a block of wood about 1 1/4 in. thick is mounted on the face-plate and is bored out with a chisel, thus forming a recess in which the cylinder can be pressed by the hand. The recess is not taken through to the face-plate, otherwise damage would be done to the turning tool. The next step is to turn a shallow recess on the end of the work, in order accurately to centre the bit. As the bit is adapted for use with a brace, it cannot be held by a drill chuck, but it is good enough to insert the squared end in the tapered hole in the tailstock mandrel, as shown in Fig. 42.

In order to prevent the bit from revolving, it is best held by a carrier which is shown more clearly in Fig. 43. This is an engineer's appliance, but the wood-turner will also find it useful when a drill or bit is used in the manner described. If a carrier is not available, a pair of gas-pliers will serve almost as well, but of course these will have to be gripped during the boring operation.

As some considerable power is required to bore say a 5/8-in. hole in end grain, the lowest ratio drive should be used.

The bit is fed slowly into the work by revolving the tailstock handwheel. When the boring operation is completed, the outside diameter is turned to the requisite size. If the work is rigidly held by the chuck the turning can be done without the support of the back centre, but, as it is highly probable that the overhanging end will vibrate slightly, it is best to turn up a cap especially to fit over the end (Fig. 44), in order that the back centre may be brought up to support the work.

The cap can be quickly made by turning up a piece of stuff between centres and parting-off close to the back centre. This will provide a cap or plug with a hole for centring. The outside diameter can now be readily turned and finished with glass-paper, and the work parted off at the position indicated in Fig. 44. It should be found that sufficient material is now left in the chuck for the lid to be turned (Fig. 45). In order to obtain a nice fit on the box, frequent tests should be made with this part towards the latter stages of the turning. Finally, the lid is parted off as indicated in Fig. 45.

Chucking and Turning Wheels. The worker is almost sure to be asked, at some time or other, to turn up a set of wheels for a toy. Plywood is suitable for this purpose. The stuff should be cut out roughly octagonal and glued to the wood facing of the face-plate with paper inserted in between, each piece of material being similarly attached to the piece below as shown in Fig. 46. In mounting the pieces, it is best to centre each independently. In turning up the periphery, the tailstock should be brought up to support the work. It might be thought satisfactory to bore through all four wheels while mounted together on the face-plate, but there is a chance that the tip of the drill will run slightly out of truth, in which case it is best to centre each wheel with a tool and drill the axle holes independently. As the wheels are separated from each other by glued paper, no difficulty should be experienced in separating each wheel after it has been drilled.

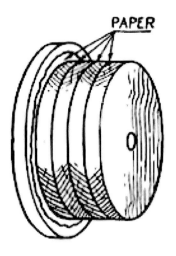

FIG. 46. WOOD GLUED UP FOR TURNING WHEELS

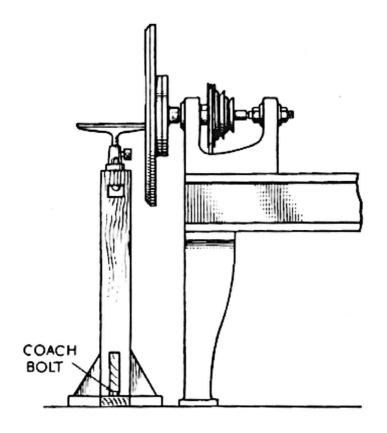

FIG. 47. TURNING LARGE WORK, HEADSTOCK
REVERSED

Turning Large Diameter Work on the Faceplate. The occasion may arise when it is desired to turn an article larger in diameter than the height of the lathe centres. If the required diameter is a little in excess of the capacity of the lathe, the headstock can be raised by a wood packing inserted between the lathe bed and the underside of the headstock. It may be that the worker wishes to turn a series of plates for a cake stand, for example, the diameter of which would make it impracticable to pack-up the headstock and use the existing belt. It will be understood that the thickness of the packing should be such that when the belt is transferred to a slower drive, as will be necessary for turning a large diameter, the belt is rightly tensioned.

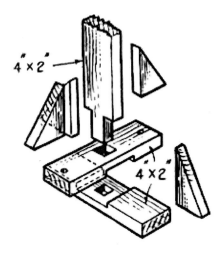

FIG. 48. BASE CONSTRUCTION OF SUPPORT
FOR T-REST

The rest is shown in position in Fig. 47.

A way out of the difficulty is to reverse the headstock, as shown in Fig. 47, so that the work will overhang the end of the lathe bed. The greatest diameter of work which can be turned in this manner will be determined by the power available which can be transmitted by the driving belt without slip. A temporary T-rest support of rigid construction will have to be made similar to that shown, the joints at the foot of the support being shown in Fig. 48. It will be necessary to secure the support to the floor with coachscrews. The attachment of the T-rest is best effected by a bolt and nut as shown, since this will permit of the adjustment and clamping of the T-rest. As the headstock is screwed on to the nose in a clockwise direction, it will be clear that the reversal of the headstock will require that the turning of the work will have to be done from the other side of the lathe. If the turning is done from the usual side, the face-plate will tend to unscrew. It will be necessary, of course, to reverse the motion of the lathe. This will present no difficulty if the lathe is power driven. A treadle lathe will require someone to do the treadling while the work is in process. The work will have to be done opposite handed to the usual position, but this should not cause any difficulty, it being assumed that the work is cut as circular as possible with a bow-saw before turning, so as to leave a minimum of work to be done on the lathe.

MISCELLANEOUS WORK BETWEEN CENTRES

IT is sometimes necessary to turn a handle with a hole running through the centre. Such a handle is shown in Fig. 49. The hole is drilled before turning as centrally in the material as possible.

Use of the Mandrel. The next step is to turn up a mandrel indicated at *g*, Fig. 49. This should have a very slight taper, and if the diameter of the hole is relatively small, say, 1/4 in., the diameter of the mandrel should be increased at that end which will be held by the fork chuck. It will be found that the tapered mandrel will give sufficient frictional grip to the work to enable it to be turned.

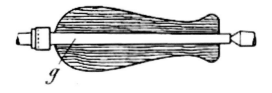

FIG. 49. WOOD MOUNTED ON A MANDREL

This method is followed when turning a
handle having a hole running through it.

Turning Bulbous Legs. In turning bulbous legs (Fig. 50), the extra material for the bulbous portion can be applied by building up the legs as shown in Fig. 53. Obviously good glued joints should be made, otherwise they will show up when the turning is completed. It is as well in built-up work to cut the stuff from one piece so that the figure more or less matches up. This can be obtained by arranging the medullary rays in the same general direction, as shown in Fig. 52, although, perhaps, it may be difficult to get the rays to accurately join up across the joints. This will assure that the figure will appear on adjoining pieces.

FIG. 50. BULBOUS LEG

FIG. 51. DOWELLED LEG

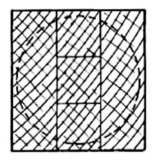

FIG. 52. SECTION THROUGH BUILT-UP LEG

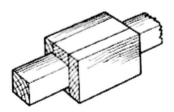

FIG. 53. WOOD BUILT UP FOR MAKING
BULBOUS LEG

Turnery that exceeds the length of the Lathe. It sometimes happens that the length of a piece of turnery, or a part having a turned portion, is greater than the maximum distance between the centres of the lathe. In such cases each portion can be made separately and secured to an adjacent part by a dowelled joint as shown in Fig. 51, the dowel being formed integral with the turned part or parts.

It will be understood that such an expedient is unsatisfactory if the turning is liable to be subjected to a transverse strain such as would occur in a chair leg. In the example given, the bulbous turning at the lower end of the leg is held rigid by the rail and thus there is little risk of a fracture occurring at the dowelled joint.

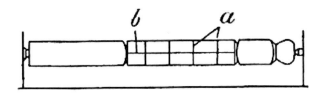

FIG. 54. PRELIMINARY MARKING FOR TWIST TURNING

FIG. 55. PRELIMINARY CUTTING AWAY OF TWIST

FIG. 56. MARKING SPIRAL WITH PAPER STRIP
GLUED ROUND

Forming a Twist in the Lathe. A worker newly possessing
a lathe will perhaps have visions of being able to turn twists,
but unfortunately, this cannot be done on an ordinary lathe.
A twist is really a quick pitch thread, and a tool carrier, such as
a slide rest, would have to move very rapidly to cut the thread,
that is if the lathe were driven at its usual wood-turning speed.
Therefore a lathe has to be specially designed for this kind of
work.

However, a lathe provides excellent means for mounting
the work while the twist is being cut by hand. The first step
is to turn up a cylinder slightly larger in diameter than that
of the required twist. The pitch, that is to say, the distance
from the top of one rounded portion to the other, in a single
twist, is generally made equal to the diameter; therefore start
at one end of the cylinder and mark pencil lines *a* round the
circumference as shown in Fig. 54, the lines being the same
distance apart as the diameter of the cylinder. These lines can
be quickly drawn by holding the pencil against the cylinder
whilst it is being rotated. Then draw a line *b* along the cylinder
parallel to the axis and, at the intersection of the lines, press in

an ordinary pin. Panel pins will make too large a hole which will show up when the work is completed. Next prepare a strip of paper about equal to one-third the pitch in width and roughly four times as long as the cylinder. Coat one side of the paper with glue and wrap it round the cylinder—as shown in Fig. 56—the nails serving as a guide for the required pitch. When the glue is dry, remove the pins and proceed to cut a V groove in the area covered by the paper, as shown in Fig. 57. Next, prepare a wooden wedge and drive it in between the headstock casting and the pulley cone. The wedge will hold the pulley cone stationary while the right hand edge of the V groove is being rounded as illustrated in Fig. 58. This is best done with a 1/2-in. chisel. As the work proceeds around the circumference of the cylinder, it will be necessary from time to time to remove the wedge and reinsert it. Having rounded one edge, remove the cylinder from the lathe and reverse it, thus bringing the unfinished edge of the groove to the right-hand side for rounding. By reversing the work in the lathe, the cutting will be done against the long fibres of the wood thus making the cutting operation easier and avoiding any possibility of the wood splintering. The wedge can now be removed and the work slowly revolved by hand whilst the bottom of the thread or twist is eased out with a gouge, and a rough finish given to the rounded portions of the twist with a rasp. The final finish is effected by the use of coarse and fine glasspaper.

FIG. 57. USING THE SAW FOR THE PRELIMINARY
CUTTING OF THE V GROOVE

WEDGE

FIG. 58. CHISELLING SIDES OF THE V GROOVE.
NOTE WEDGE TO HOLD WORK STILL

Double Twist. The marking-out of a double twist is
shown in Fig. 59. As in the single twist, circumferential lines
are marked around the diameter at a distance apart equal to
the diameter, but in this case two parallel lines are drawn
diametrically opposite to each other. At the intersection
of these lines with those passing around the cylinder are
positioned pins. Two strips of paper are then wound around
the cylinder. In Fig. 59, one of the strips is shown in black
and the other by shaded lines and it will be noticed that these
strips contact every other pin and that each forms a thread

having a pitch equal to twice the diameter of the cylinder. By using these proportions, a pleasing twist results, but it will be understood that the pitch can be varied as desired.

FIG. 59. STRIPS OF PAPER USED TO MARK
DOUBLE TWIST

FIG. 60. DOUBLE TWIST HOLES SHOW HOW
BINES ARE SEPARATED

The quicker pitch provided by a double twist is an advantage in working, since the fibres are cut at a smaller angle relatively to the axis than is the case with a single twist; consequently less effort is required in paring the twist to shape. This will be apparent on referring to Figs. 59 and 60.

FIG. 61. OPEN DOUBLE BINE TWIST

FIG. 62. OPEN TRIPLE BINE TWIST

A pleasing effect can be obtained by separating the strands of a double twist as shown in Fig. 61. This is done by boring a series of holes, as indicated in Fig. 60, and then paring the work so that the strands are separated, finishing with a rasp and glasspaper.

Triple Twist. An even more satisfactory result can be

obtained with a triple twist, as illustrated in Fig. 62. In marking-out the triple twist, three strips of paper would be necessary and the pitch would be equal to three times the diameter of the cylinder, that is, if this proportion is used. The two designs illustrated lend themselves very well to candlesticks or to table lamp standards.

Turning a Ball. The worker may, at some time or other, desire to turn a ball. Now, to produce a ball which is a true sphere presents some little difficulty, especially in regard to holding the work. One way in which a fairly accurate ball may be formed is to turn first a cylinder, the length of which is about three times the diameter of the ball. Out of this cylinder will be formed the ball, a bell chuck for holding the work, and a pad for fitting over the centre. The next step is to shape the cylinder as shown in Fig. 63. The zone y should be turned as accurately as possible to the required diameter and curvature of the ball, leaving, however, a little for cleaning off with glasspaper.

In order to obtain accuracy it will be necessary to employ a template (Fig. 64), for testing the surface. This can be made from cardboard or thin metal. The diameter x of the part A, which will be used later as a chuck, is made equal to y. The stem s is taper-turned to a diameter which will enable the stem to be wedged in the central hole in the lathe mandrel or a hole in a block fastened to the faceplate. When shaping the zones *z* care should be taken to make the curves a little flatter than that of zone *y*. Thus when the ball portion B is parted off the diameter *d* is full.

Before parting off, a pencil line should be marked on the diameter as indicated. This line is, in fact, what is known in geometry as a great circle. The parts A, B, and C are now parted off, and the chuck portion is inserted tightly into the lathe mandrel or hole in the block and turned as shown in Fig. 65. It will be noted that the radius of the inside curve of the chuck is less than that of the ball so that contact with the ball will be made at the rim. When separating the pad portion C, the parting tool should be inclined so that the pad is undercut, as shown in Fig. 66. It is not possible to do this without leaving a central pip, but this can be cut away after the pad is parted off.

The chuck having been prepared, the ball is mounted as shown in Fig. 67, with the pad engaging the back centre. It will be seen that the ball is arranged so that the pencil line is horizontal and that the finished zone *y* is in engagement with the chuck. Before proceeding further, a drop of oil should be placed on the back centre. Light cuts are then taken over the surface, removing the wood to the pencil line but never obliterating it. This, if carefully done, should result in a ball which is spherical to all intents and purposes. It may be necessary to make one or two adjustments of the ball in the chuck in order to true up the zone about *m*, but if the rule never to cut beyond the pencil line is observed, the adjustment will have no ill effect.

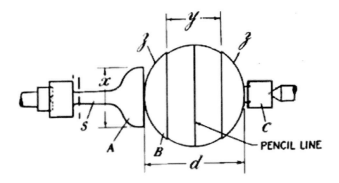

FIG. 63. TURNING A BALL. PRELIMINARY
SHAPING

FIG. 64. TEMPLATE USED IN TURNING A BALL

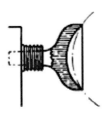

FIG. 65. CHUCK A HOLDING BALL

FIG. 66. PAD C. NOTE HOW END IS UNDERCUT

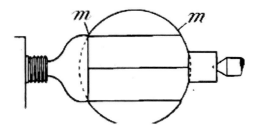

FIG. 67. BALL HELD BETWEEN CHUCK A AND PAD C FOR FINAL TURNING

If a number of balls are required, the chuck and pad are made with the first ball, the other balls being turned a little oval with a central zone accurately shaped for fitting in the chuck and resting against the pad. Special ball-turning tools having a concave edge agreeing with certain diameters of balls can be obtained, but these are not essential. The work can be done satisfactorily with the gouge and chisel.

SPLIT TURNINGS, TURNED MOULDINGS, AND SQUARE TURNING

FIG. 68. SPLIT TURNING

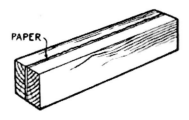

FIG. 69. SPLIT TURNING WOOD

Two pieces are glued together with paper
between to enable them to be separated.

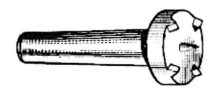

FIG. 70. DRIVING SPUR

The use of this avoids liability of joint to
open when making a split turning.

JACOBEAN split turnings were largely used in furniture of
that period, and in modern reproductions of furniture in the
style a pleasing result can be obtained if such decoration is
used with restraint. It would appear that a split turning, as
illustrated in Fig. 68, could be turned and then cut through
its length. This is not so simple as it seems, owing to the
difficulty in holding the work while sawing and afterwards

planing the sawn surfaces.

Preparing the Work. A more satisfactory method is to glue two pieces of stuff together with paper in between (Fig. 69). The centres are then marked by drawing the diagonal lines at each end, taking care that each centre is on the joint of the two pieces. There is a danger that if a fork chuck is used it may open the glued joint. It is therefore advisable to use a driving spur (Fig. 70), if possible.

Separating and Finishing the Turnings. On completing the turning, the halves are separated by sliding the blade of a table knife down the glued joint. The back of each split turning should be found to be true and level but each will have paper adhering to it. This can be removed by rubbing each turning on a piece of glasspaper laid on a level surface such as the lathe bed.

Turned Mouldings. It is possible to turn decorative mouldings in a lathe, a suitable design for a moulding formed in this manner being shown in section (Fig. 71). As such mouldings are generally required in a length greater than that between the centres of a lathe, it can be arranged to turn several lengths simultaneously within the capacity of the lathe and then place these lengths end to end in order to make up the total length required.

Method of Working. A core of pine or deal is trued up, taking care that it is as square as possible in cross section. The length of the core should be such that it will just go between the lathe centres. The strips of wood which are to form the mouldings are next prepared. Two of these strips should be equal in width to the core, whilst the other two strips are made equal to the width of the core plus twice the thickness of the strips.

FIG. 71. TURNED MOULDING

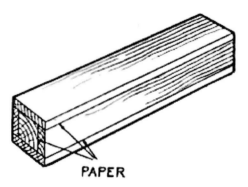

PAPER

FIG. 72. HOW WOOD FOR TURNED MOULDING
IS GLUED TO CENTRE CORE

The strips thus prepared are now glued to the core, paper being inserted in the joints. The core with the strips mounted on it ready for turning is shown in Fig. 72. When marking the centres at the ends of the core care should be taken to see that each centre is accurately located. The wood is then chucked and turned cylindrical as indicated in Fig. 73, after which operation the beads are formed, as shown towards the left-hand end of Fig. 73.

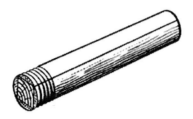

FIG. 73. HOW MOULDING IS TURNED ON A
CENTRE CORE

FIG. 74. MOULDING SEPARATED FROM CORE

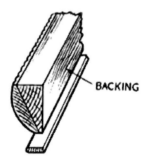

FIG. 75. MOULDING GLUED TO BACKING

Finally, the turned mouldings are removed with a table knife in the manner previously described. If the work has been done carefully, the result should be four similar mouldings, each as shown in Fig. 74, making it possible for the lengths of mouldings to be butted together to form one long length. In some cases it may be necessary to mount the mouldings permanently on a pine or deal backing as shown in Fig. 75.

Quasi-square Turning. It is possible to turn articles square, or more strictly speaking, quasis-quare, on a lathe, a sample of such turning being shown in Fig. 76. This would appear to be something in the nature of a paradox, but it can be done. The method employed is to turn up a, large diameter drum *a* (Fig. 77), having cheeks *b* and mounted on a steel shaft. At the headstock end, the drum is attached to the face-plate, the shaft being central at the other end on the tailstock. The pieces of wood to be square turned are planed up true and square and are cut to length so that they will fit tightly between the cheeks of the drum, each piece being of such size that when all are mounted on the periphery of the drum they will fit tightly.

In order to hold the pieces firmly in place, a steel strap is passed around each end, being clamped by a bolt and wing nut. Fig. 77 shows one of these straps in position. The pieces thus mounted are turned to the required shape, after which the straps are removed and each piece given a quarter turn and the straps replaced. This procedure is repeated until all faces are turned. The turning of the last face may give some difficulty since the fibres on the far edge of the work are now unsupported and will tend to break away during the cutting operation. This can be largely avoided by taking shearing cuts wherever possible.

The process is described because it may be of interest, but it is unlikely that the lathe of the average worker will allow sufficient swing to permit of a barrel being turned of a diameter which would give substantially square turnings. It is obvious that unless the drum is relatively large, the turned faces will be conspicuously curved.

FIG. 76. EXAMPLE OF SQUARE TURNING

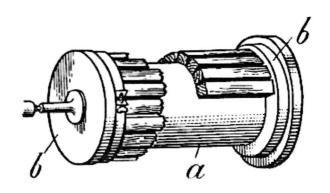

FIG. 77. WOOD FIXED TO DRUM FOR SQUARE
TURNING

FLOOR LAMP STANDARD AND TABLE LAMP BORING

IT might be thought that a turned column for a floor standard lamp would be beyond the capacity of the lathe possessed by the average worker. This is true only if the column is formed in one piece. It is possible, however, to build up the column from several turned sections, each being of a length which will permit its being mounted between centres. They are secured together by pin and socket joints.

Making the Column in sections. Fig. 78 shows a standard lamp built up from three sections, *a, b*, and *c*, the parts being joined together by pins and sockets as shown enlarged. The pins are turned with the sections and the sockets bored with a twist bit. If it can be contrived to bore the sockets in the lathe, so much the better, as the aligning of the sections will be assured. Oak, mahogany, and beech are satisfactory woods for the lamp, though beech will require staining. As the boring of the central hole for the flex is a difficult and tedious job, it is best to rip the stuff for each section through the centre and work a semi-circular plough groove in each half for the wiring hole. This should be about 3/8 in. diameter, not less. The sawn faces are trued up and the halves glued together. It will be necessary to plug the wiring hole temporarily in each section at the ends in order accurately to centre the work in the lathe. The centred plugs will also enable the sockets to be bored truly central. The plugs in the pin ends will, of course, have to be bored out on completion of the turning.

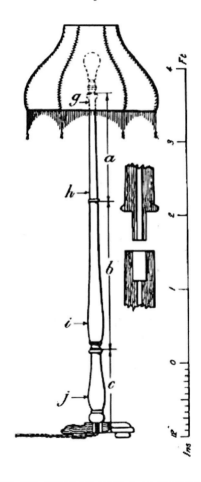

FIG. 78. STANDARD LAMP DESIGN

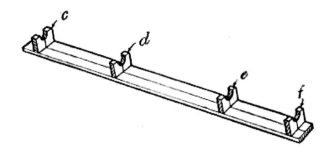

FIG. 79. CRADLE FOR ASSEMBLING THE
STANDARD

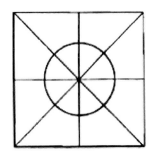

FIG. 80. HOW CRADLE SUPPORTS ARE SET OUT

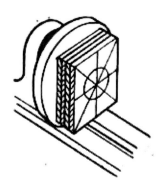

FIG. 81. TURNING CRADLE SUPPORTS

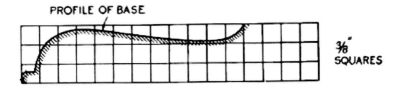

PROFILE OF BASE

¾" SQUARES

FIG. 82. SHAPE OF BASE SET OUT IN SQUARES

Assembling the Column. In order that the three sections should be held in alignment while the glue is setting, it is advisable to make up a cradle for the support of the assembled column as shown in Fig. 79. The positions of the supports *c, d, e,* and *f* are optional but they are shown as corresponding to the diameters *g, h, i* and *j,* Fig. 78. The four supports are formed from 3/8-in. stuff and all are cut carefully square and equal in size. One of the squares is set out as shown in Fig. 80 and all four are glued together with paper in between and mounted on the face-plate, the marked-out piece being placed outside (Fig. 81).

This piece is bored out equal to diameter *g* and is then removed and sawn through the centre, forming two similar halves, one of which is used as a support. The operation is repeated in turn with each piece, boring out holes equal to diameters *h, i,* and *j* respectively. In order to assure the aligned assembly of the supports with the base, the latter is gauged through its centre and a line squared centrally of each support. If the supports are now mounted so that the lines coincide, they should be found to be accurately aligned. They should of course be square with the edge of the base.

Turning the Base. The suggested diameter of the base, shown in profile in Fig. 82, is 12 ins. This may be too large for the lathe unless the latter is gapped. It may therefore be necessary to reverse the headstock and turn the base from the end of the lathe as described in a previous chapter. The centre hole in the base to receive the bottom pin of the standard should be bored on the lathe. This will ensure that the column will be square with the base and consequently will stand perpendicularly.

The pin securing the column to the base should be sawn through its diameter to allow the insertion of a wedge. This is glued in place and afterwards bored out for the flex.

Drilling the Long Central Holes. It is by no means an easy task to drill the central hole in a table lamp, for example. Owing to the length of the stem portion, the drilling has to be done from both ends and, unless the worker is fairly skilful, the chances are that the holes will not meet. The possession of a lathe enables this drilling operation to be done with ease and accuracy. In turning the stem portion of the lamp, the waste wood at the tailstock end should be turned, say slightly under 3/4 in. diameter. The stem is then removed and fitted in the base, which should be still mounted on the face-plate as shown in Fig. 83. Even if the stem fits tightly and is accurately centred, the unsupported end may revolve slightly out of truth.

For the purpose of drilling, this unsupported end is held in a saddle as shown. This comprises two pieces of wood fixed together, the upright piece having a hole in which the projecting end of the stem revolves. The saddle is clamped to the lathe bed by a bolt and nut, the nut being tightened against a strip of wood under the lathe bed. The precise position for the hole in the saddle can be ascertained by clamping the saddle down and then moving up the tailstock so that a mark can be made by the back centre. It is advisable to make a pencil mark on the saddle coinciding with the edge of the lathe bed, in order that the saddle may be positioned correctly transversely.

With the work mounted and supported by the saddle, the depression in the stem in which the back centre was positioned is enlarged by a tool to the diameter of the required hole, say 5/16 in. This done, an auger should be mounted as shown, the tool being rested in semi-circular recesses formed in supports as shown. The support nearest the tailstock is fixed similarly to the saddle. The purpose of these supports is to assure that the auger will remain in alignment with the axis of the stem during the drilling operation.

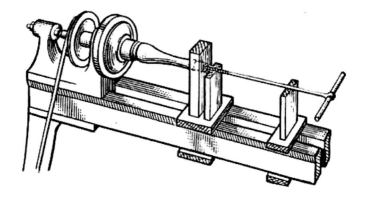

FIG. 83. DRILLING THE WIRING HOLE IN A
LAMP STANDARD

Note how the saddles keep the bit in
alignment.

Another Method of Drilling. An alternative method is
to mount a twist drill in the lathe between the back centre
and the centre mark in the lamp stem. The drill is then fed
into the work by rotating the tailstock handwheel. The drill
must, of course, be held against rotation. This can be done by
attaching a carrier to the drill, as is done by the engineer, and
the carrier rested on the T-rest. If the worker does not possess
a carrier, the drill can be held by a pair of gas pliers. The drill,
most probably, will not be long enough to penetrate the work,
but as the greater part of the hole can thus be bored, it should
not be difficult to drill from the opposite end and get the
holes to meet, when the work is removed from the lathe.

SIMPLE LATHE CONSTRUCTION

A WORKER, with a little ingenuity, can make a perfectly serviceable lathe. The only real difficulty is the headstock, which necessitates a turned pulley fixed to a shaft or mandrel which is so mounted in bearings that adjustment for any slackness can be made. A satisfactory way of overcoming the difficulty of the headstock construction is to use the rear hub of a discarded cycle wheel for the bearing. It is best to use one from a racing cycle, if possible, as the rear hub of this kind of cycle has a longer spindle than usual and the cones are supplied with thin lock-nuts. This makes available about 3/4 in. of spindle at one end for the attachment of a pulley and a similar amount at the other end to form a nose. The lathe described is shown in Fig. 84 and is adapted to be driven by a 1/3-h.p. motor. It is obvious that one speed only is possible, but much good work, of not too ambitious a character, can be done on this simple lathe.

FIG. 84. PRACTICAL HOME-MADE LATHE WITH
HEADSTOCK BEARING MADE FROM A CYCLE HUB

Construction is straightforward though accuracy in
workmanship is essential. If a reliable hardwood is not
available a good quality deal can be used for the lathe-
bed and head- and tailstock.

Lathe-bed Construction. The material for the bed should
be carefully trued up as the accuracy of the lathe depends
on careful workmanship. The length of the bed is not given
as this is governed by the required length between centres.
The bed is supported by two feet, each having a tenon which
is fitted in slots cut in the bed. In order that the headstock
shall be rigidly attached to the bed it is secured to the latter
by means of a lapped joint. The next step therefore is to slot
the two parts of the bed for the feet and headstock. At the
headstock end a slot is made in each part of the bed equal in
width to the headstock and the thickness of the adjacent foot.

The construction of the feet can be left until the headstock is fitted as it will then be possible to ascertain the exact size of the tenon on each foot.

Headstock Construction. This part is formed from one piece of timber. After truing up, the cross-grooves are made at the lower end. Care should be taken to see that they are square with the headstock. The headstock- is then assembled with the bed, and the joint forced up tightly in the vice and two 1/4-in. holes are bored for the bolts *b*, shown in Fig. 84. A 1/4-in. hole is also bored to take the bolt *c*, and a hole to take a 3 in. wood screw at *d*.

The distance between the inner faces of the two flanges, through which the spokes are threaded on the cycle hub, is next measured, and a rebate is cut out of the headstock as shown at *e*. Next gauge a line *f*, Fig. 85 (A) all round the headstock and also square a line indicating the bearing centre. This done, saw the headstock in halves on line *f* and clean the sawn surfaces. The two halves are then placed together and fixed tightly with the bolt *c* and screw *d*. At this stage a hole, just large enough to take the middle portion of the hub, is bored at the intersection of the central saw cut and the squared line. It will be found that an adjustable bit is useful for this purpose. It may be necessary to recess the ends of the hole as shown at *g*, Fig. 85 (B).

The headstock can now be taken apart and the hub fitted.

It may be necessary to ease the hole slightly with a rasp but the hub should be a tight fit. The oil filler cap in the spindle will have to be removed and a 1/4 in. hole *h*, Fig. 85 (B), is bored in the position shown. To ensure that the oil hole coincides with the hole *h*, two screws should be inserted in the headstock through the spoke holes. The headstock may now be assembled with the bed and all bolts well tightened, washers being placed under the nuts. The top wood screw is of course screwed home tightly.

It will now be possible to arrive at the required width of the tenon on each foot. With the dimensions given, the gap in the bed should be about 1 in. The two feet are best prepared in one length of stuff and afterwards sawn in two. The tenons should be cut carefully as they also serve as distance pieces, ensuring a uniform gap in the lathe bed. The feet are secured by bolts similarly to the headstock. The two buttons (Fig. 84), when turned down, project beyond the bottom of the feet and rest against the front edge of the bench to prevent the lathe being pushed away from the worker when in use.

Tailstock Construction. The tailstock is made from a block of wood 9 3/4 in. by 4 in. by 3 in. This has a tenon 1 3/4 in. in depth and of a thickness which permits the tailstock to slide freely without side play.

The back centre is made from a 1/2-in. Whitworth bolt 7 in. long with a hexagonal head. The thread on the bolt should extend up to the head. It would be best to have the point turned, but if this is not possible it can be filed. The handle is formed from a short piece of 1/4-in. iron rod, threaded 1/4-in. Whitworth at one end and bent at right angles. A 3/16-in. hole is bored transversely through the bolt head and tapped 1/4 in. Whitworth. The handle is then screwed into the hole.

In order to locate the position of the back centre, the tailstock can be brought up to the live centre and pressed against it. This will leave an indentation from which the centre can be fairly accurately determined. A 3/4-in. hole is then bored to take the tailstock screw. For the adjustment of the screw, two iron plates, each drilled and tapped 1/2-in. Whitworth, are secured to the back and front of the tailstock by wood screws.

The method of clamping the tailstock to the bed is illustrated in Fig. 85 (C). A 3/8-in. hole is bored up the centre of the tenon to a distance of about 5 in. A square 1/2-in. Whitworth nut is then sunk into the face of the tailstock so that it is fixed over the 3/8-in. hole and at a distance of about 3 1/4 ins. from the extreme end of the tenon. A 5 in. by 1/2 in. square-headed Whitworth bolt has a large washer placed on it and is screwed up into the nut in the tailstock from under the lathe bed. A handle for ease in tightening the bolt can be made in the same way as suggested for the back centre, but for greater convenience it should project from both sides of the bolt head. Alternatively a wing nut could be used, in which case the bolt head would be unnecessary.

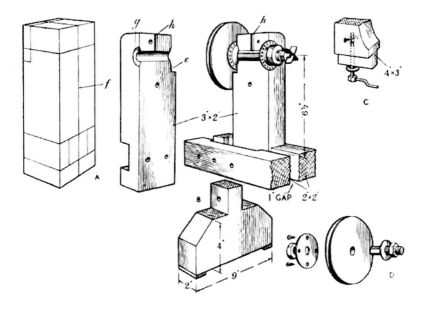

FIG. 85. CONSTRUCTION DETAILS

A Shows marking out of timber for headstock. B gives method of mounting hub in the headstock. C Method of fixing tailstock in the bed. D Pulley fixing.

The Tool Rest. The base can be formed from thick plywood and is slotted to take a 1/2-in. Whitworth round-head bolt. Clamping is effected by a large washer against which a wing-nut is tightened.

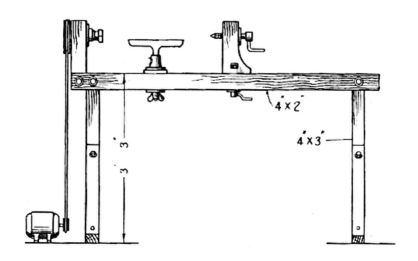

FIG. 86. LATHE MOUNTED UPON STANDARDS

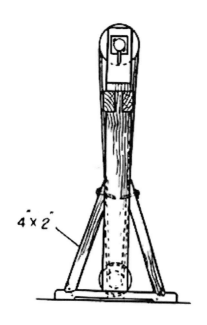

FIG. 87. END ELEVATION OF LATHE

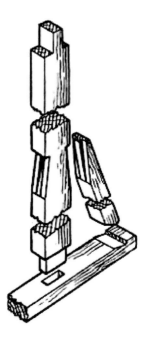

FIG. 88. CONSTRUCTION OF THE STANDARDS

The metal base for the rest can be formed from a 1 in. steam flange in which a tube is welded. This tube is drilled and tapped to take a clamping screw. The actual rest will have to be made by a blacksmith. It comprises a piece of steel 9 in. by 1 1/2 in. by 3/8 in. welded to a rod which should be a sliding fit on the tube.

The live centre is made from two strips of iron 1 1/4 ins. by 1/2 in. No. 14 gauge, halved together at the centre and soldered into slots cut in a cycle hub nut of the type used on the chain side of a Sturmey Archer 3-speed gear.

The lathe pulley can be made on the lathe. This can be done by first preparing a temporary pulley cut out with the bow saw and a groove worked on its periphery with a gouge. This rough pulley serves to drive the lathe while the permanent pulley is being turned. The material for the permanent pulley, which should be hardwood, is cut roughly circular and mounted on the live centre, where it is clamped by a nut. The rough disc can then be turned truly circular and a groove cut to take a 3/8-in. circular belt. A suitable size for the pulley is 4 1/2 in. diameter by 1/2 in. thick.

It may be found that a nut is ineffective in clamping the driving pulley to the spindle when large diameters are being turned. It may therefore be necessary to key the pulley to the shaft. This can be done in a simple manner as shown in Fig. 85 (D). As the spindle will be formed of hardened steel, it will be necessary to grind the flat surface.

Some accessories for the lathe will be found necessary. A face-plate can be made from an iron disc about 1/2 in. thick. The centre tapped hole for screwing the plate on the nose of the lathe will have to be bored and tapped on a metal-turning lathe as it is essential that the hole should be truly central and square with the face of the plate.

A sandpapering disc is also useful, as is also a carborundum grinding wheel. This can be clamped to the live centre by a nut.

The dimension 6 1/2 in. from the centres to the bed can be made less if so desired, but if it is increased to enable work of greater diameter to be mounted, it may be found that the power available is insufficient.

Mounting the Lathe on Standards. The lathe described can be mounted on standards, as shown in Figs. 86 and 87. This will necessitate the bed terminating flush with the end of the headstock so that the belt drive will not be obstructed by the bed. In the previous construction the motor is fixed to the bench and no hindrance is caused to the belt by the bed. In place of the feet, two standards are fitted, the construction of which is shown in Fig. 88. The standards should be perfectly rigid, and in order that they should remain so, the fixing of the parts should be effected by coach screws and bolts as indicated. This will enable the parts to be tightened should they work loose owing to vibration.

In the construction of the bench lathe, the size of the bed was given as 2 ins. by 2 ins., but for the purpose of obtaining a good fixing to the standards it would be an advantage to increase the depth of the bed to 4 ins.

In order that the belt may be tightened, it is as well to mount the motor so that its position may be adjusted. This may be done by mounting the motor on battens screwed to the floor and having slots for the holding-down bolts.

POLISHING WORK ON THE LATHE

WORKERS who are able to french polish flat surfaces satisfactorily may not have the same success with turned articles. It would appear that, as the work can be rotated in the lathe, the several processes in french polishing would be facilitated. But the fact that work can be revolved quickly introduces a difficulty, since if the speed is too great the stain will not penetrate properly into the pores of the wood and when polish is being applied the excessive friction may spoil the work.

Legs and other turned pieces which are to be lathe polished should be left of sufficient length so that the centre marks which are made by the mandrel and the tailstock can be retained until the work is practically completed. The work should also have a "tally" mark to enable the turner to take the work out of the lathe and re-centre it in its original position at any later period. This is important because the work has to be constantly taken out of the lathe to allow it to dry, and in due course it has to be re-chucked or centred to glasspaper the surface.

The Stains used may be either water or oil; the latter penetrate more deeply into the wood and do not raise the grain as much as a water stain. Admittedly the oil stains take longer to dry, but they give a nice effect upon birch, beech, ash, oak, and the lighter coloured woods.

Whatever type of stain be used it is necessary that the turned work be damped down with, warm water, thoroughly dried and re-chucked and glasspapered down with No. 1 or No. 0 grade paper before any stain is applied. It is obvious that any square stock (as for legs or pillars) is more or less "quartered" on two of its edges, and when turned, some of the wood will show more or less the end way of the grain according to the contour of the turning. There will therefore be a decided difference in the amount of grain raising, and this must be carefully eradicated by the sanding process.

The Sanding should not be done by revolving the turning in one direction. This has a tendency to rub the fibres down and give a false impression of smoothness. The revolution of the lathe should occasionally be reversed so that the loose fibres will be "wiped up" and then be removed by the glasspaper.

After the grain raising and sanding has been satisfactorily accomplished the work is ready for staining, and the stain may be applied with either a sponge, a piece of old flannel, or a brush. Vandyke water stain for mid-brown Jacobean oak is best applied with a brush. The strap may be thrown off the lathe and the mandrel revolved by hand during the staining operation so as to ensure a slow speed. The stain will require well brushing in, because the open pores always appear to be greasy, and unless the stain is allowed to dry into the wood for about three minutes, the work will show the unstained pores.

Use the stain freely, and, after it has stood a few minutes, wipe off the surplus liquid with a rag whilst the lathe is treadled slowly. Be sure to wipe well into the arrises or corners of the quirks or turnings. The rag may be held upon the work so as to cover two-thirds of the diameter, as when polishing the household tap.

On completion take out the turning and put it aside to dry whilst you stain the next leg of the series. For mahogany and baywood turnings use a water solution of bichromate of potash as a stain. In the first instance use it weak enough, because the end grain of the turning will take the stain a shade darker than the other portions. Allow the work to dry, and, if thought necessary, give the light portions of the work another wipe with the stain so as to obtain an even tone.

Turned work in walnut does not as a rule require any staining, but it is usual to wipe on to it a little raw linseed oil to bring out the figure. Oiling, however, always slightly darkens the wood, and it will therefore be at the discretion of the worker as to the advisability of oiling or leaving the work un-oiled according to the colour of the carcase work which it is intended to match.

Whatever stain is used it is advisable after the stain has

dried to replace the work in the lathe and, whilst it is slowly revolving, give it a brush coating of thin french polish, about 4 ozs. to the pint, which will seal the stain into the pores of the wood. When dry, wipe the work very sparingly with linseed oil and re-glasspaper the turning with No. 0, taking great care not to cut through the stain. Next friction polish the work with a dry rag.

Polishing. The work may now be finished by repeated applications at suitable intervals of wax polish, driving the lathe first in one direction and then in the other, and brushing the wax compound out of the small members of the mouldings. To obtain a french-polished surface the wood will have to be repeatedly brush-coated with thin french polish and sanded down until the pores are well filled up.

At this stage apply a little polish on a pad of cotton wadding which is covered with a fine piece of rag, the face of which has been anointed with a spot of white vaseline oil. The rubber must be soft so that it can be moulded to the intricacy of the various shapes, and the work must be revolved very slowly— not more than, say, sixty revolutions per minute.

Proceed to body up the turnings in this manner, allowing them at intervals to dry out. When the pores are filled up and a good body appears on the work, place it aside over-night to harden off and sink. Re-chuck the work and apply a slight touch of polish in the same way as when originally bodying the work. When this bodying is completed give the whole of the work a light and quick rub with a new polishing rubber which is very slightly charged with methylated spirits only. After this, wipe the turnings with a soft cloth such as a piece of butter muslin.

Prepare this rag as follows. The night before it is required place into an air-tight lever tin a piece of cotton wadding on which you have sprinkled about a tablespoonful of methylated spirits. Fold your rag to a convenient pad and place it on top of the wadding. Then close the tin and leave it to stand overnight. On opening the tin it will be observed that the rag has absorbed sufficient dampness from the cotton wadding to act as a burnishing rubber. Turned work of small diameter, say, up to 2 ins., is filled in by repeated applications of brush polish which is sanded and levelled up in the lathe. For turnings of large diameter, such as billiard table legs, it is usual to fill up the grain with a suitable coloured grain-filling paste. Bear in mind that the filler for turned work should be slightly lighter in shade than that used for the carcase work.

When using polish for mahogany jobs it is necessary to tint slightly the orange polish with a spot of bismarck aniline dye; otherwise the coating of orange polish will appear muddy and out of keeping with the warm tone of the stained mahogany. Lastly, guard against the risk of running the lathe at too great a speed. If your treadle is fitted with a small driving wheel for turning metal, by all means make use of it for polishing woodwork; otherwise rotate the mandrel at a very slow speed, either by a special gear or by revolving the mandrel head by hand. The principal use of the lathe is for rubbing the work down and not applying the french polish.

Oak. A pleasing finish can be obtained by wax polishing. The polish can be prepared by placing white wax in a saucer over a receptacle containing water which is then boiled. This will have the effect of melting the wax, and to the melted wax turpentine is added. When cold, the compound should resemble one of the well-known floor pastes. The compound is rubbed well into the work, and in this case the lathe is revolved rapidly in order that as much friction as possible is applied, the application of the wax being effected with a cotton or linen rag, or better still, a stiff brush. The lathe is revolved first one way and then the other, the wax being brushed out of all the quirks and sunk fillets. Much labour can be saved by bodying-in all of the turned work before framing any carcase portion of the work, as for instance where a number of chair or table legs is concerned.

Lightning Source UK Ltd.
Milton Keynes UK
UKOW03f0323160914

238635UK00001B/35/P